# QUICK AND DIRTY SECRETS OF COLLEGE SUCCESS – A PROFESSOR TELLS IT ALL

Blue Boy Publishing Company
Camillus, NY.

*To learn more about Dr. Watkins' seminars or to gain more information, visit:*

www.boycewatkins.com

Visit the author's website at:
www.boycewatkins.com

For more information or to find out how to participate in one of Dr. Watkins' seminars on college success, you can send email to info@boycewatkins.com, or call (315) 487-1176.

Dr. Watkins' other titles:

*Everything you ever wanted to know about college – a guide for minority students*

*The parental 411- what every parent should know about their child in college.*

Organizations, schools and universities can receive substantial bulk discounts by ordering 50 or more copies from the publisher. Also, groups may use the books for fund-raisers by introducing them to your members and/or parents. For more details, please call (315) 487-1176, or email info@boycewatkins.com

ISBN: 0-9742632-1-4

Cover by Jonathan Gullery at Budget Book Design

# DEDICATION

My grandmother taught me to watch every
cent
My mother taught me that school pays the
rent
My father taught me how to be strong
My Uncles taught me how not to do wrong

My aunties taught me how to have fun
My sister's the sweetest chick under the sun
My brother taught me to love all my kin
For he's not just my brother, he's my very
best friend

I love each of you with all my heart, lungs
and kidneys.

To my best friend Greg, may you rest in
peace.

# Table of contents

# All that other stuff that we haven't talked about already

# Welcome!

Welcome to the world of college! I am going to tell you a lot of stuff. This book is going to give you the opportunity to learn from my experiences as a professor and student, mistakes I've made and from what I've learned through other people and sources.

I was successful as a student, but I have had many more failures than successes. Most wise people will tell you that the path to success is typically paved with failure. When you try to do something very difficult and worthwhile, you are usually going to take a lot of hard knocks to get to the finish line. Many times, you will never reach what you sought in the first place. But think about it: if it were easy to get, would it be valuable? No! If you could become a doctor by going to school 3 weeks, then everyone in the country would be a doctor, and they would probably earn about less money than a fast food worker. So, even though it is tough to make it through medical school, doctors are glad that it was hard for them, because it gave them a chance to distinguish themselves from the pack.

When I went to college and graduate school, I was usually the only black person in my class. In fact, I never had *one single black professor all through college and many years of graduate school*. I sometimes failed tests, I received bad grades from time to time, and there were periods when I endured intense humiliation. But I persisted, and you know what happened? When I finished my PhD, I was the *only graduating African-American Finance PhD in the world to finish their degree that year.* This was a great honor and an achievement, but it was painful to get there.

So, do I feel like a successful person? Sometimes. But honestly, I didn't always feel successful. Many times, I feel like a complete failure, because I've tried to do something many times and failed each time. But I always remember something that is very important: If I keep trying, I will continue to get better. After a while, what used to be impossible will become easy. That is how life works for those who are able to overcome their obstacles.

You should understand that starting college is an amazing opportunity. It is the beginning of the next stage of your life and an opportunity for you to make your dreams come true. It can also be an opportunity for you to make your worst nightmares come true. It's really up to you.

This book contains a set of stories, rules and corny little rhymes (I used to want to be a rapper) to describe the college experience, everything from how to study to how to get financial aid. I hope that you will read this book carefully and think everything through, for all this information is here to help you. The information is presented to be brief, not detailed. My other titles (listed below) present a more complicated view of things, featuring different opinions and perspectives. This book is meant to be a "Quick and dirty" reference guide that a busy student can use to keep themselves on course as they begin and complete their college careers.

If you would like more information on these topics, you can try going to my website at www.boycewatkins.com. Also, minority students, or any student who wants a more detailed perspective than that presented here may want to read my book *Everything you ever wanted to know about college – a guide for minority students.* Parents wanting more information on how they can be involved in the college process can read *The Parental 411 – what every parent should know about their child in college.* The last book I mentioned is a guide to parents on how you can best support your child when they go to college. Parents and kids have to work together in order to make the college process a successful one. But this requires that both parties do their part.

# Who am I?

In school, I was not known for doing my
best
I was more like someone a cop would arrest

You think I was a genius? Then your
bubble will burst
I was not the best student, I was surely the
worst

It wasn't that I was a dummy you see
I just couldn't see what school did for ME

My mother became kind of concerned
When the teacher said I was unable to learn

They told her that I was a menace, a threat
"Mrs. Watkins, your boy is as bad as it
gets!"

When I was a senior, I even had sex
"Honey, I'm pregnant" is what I heard next

Right when I'm trying to buy diapers and
bibs
My father said "It's time to get out of my
crib"

18-years old with no future to boot
Man I couldn't even afford my birthday suit

So, I said to myself "Let's give college a try"
Did I think I would make it? Well, do pigs really fly?

But going to college, a fresh and new place
Was cool cuz my homies were out of my face

I wasn't distracted, so I focused on school
I made friends that were positive, not acting a fool

I also found out that school is the key
To make your world what YOU want it to be

You can buy stuff for your kids, live the fabulous life
A 6-bedroom mansion and bling bling for your wife

At some point in our lives, we all have to work hard
Whether in a nice office or in somebody's yard

The thing that will keep your back out of pain
Is how much you decide to put in your brain

## My friend Angela

I had a friend in college, lets call her Angela. She and I were very good friends as Freshmen, but I was not in her league. Angela had been in the "Who's who" of high school students, she had an incredibly high score on the ACT and SAT, and she had a 4.0 GPA during her Senior year, before enrolling at our university. She majored in some kind of complex type of biology that I never heard of, and said that afterward, she would become a neurosurgeon. I fully expected her to reach her goals. She was an incredibly focused and confident student, with the ability to reach the stars.

The first semester didn't go so well for Angela. I think that she thought that she was going to do well in college just because high school had gone so well for her. After all, you would expect a valedictorian to have no problem with the freshman year! She thought that because she was bright, she didn't have to study as hard as everyone else. Myself, on the other hand, had never made good grades, so I was scared to death. I studied as hard as I could, and got the first 4.0 GPA of my life. Angela's grades weren't bad, but this was the first time in her life she had to stare down at a report card full of Bs and Cs. She really didn't know how to take it.

One day, I saw Angela after class. She told me that she was going to move off campus, since it was cheaper. She also said that she was going to reduce her course load to about 2/3 of what it was before. I asked her why, and she said that it was because she felt that she could save money by moving away and taking fewer classes. I just nodded and said "Good luck!"

I then started to see Angela less and less. I also noticed that when I would see her, something would always be different: maybe a new tattoo here or there, or she would start smoking cigarettes or drinking more. She was still the same person in some ways, but in other ways, I could tell that she had lost her innocence. She no longer expected to make straight As, but had instead gotten used to seeing the little curly Cs and even some Ds on her report card.

She informed me about a year later that she was going to take a semester off from school. When I asked her why, she again said "To save money." I told her that I didn't think it was such a good idea, but she insisted that it was what she needed to do to "get her head together."

Eventually, I only saw Angela about once every six months. I would see her blond hair bobbing down the street toward my dorm, and I knew that she was coming to visit me. I was always happy to see her, but I worried about her. She was "kicking it" with the wrong people, and didn't seem to worried about studying. She had changed a lot from the motivated student that she was when I met her.

Eventually, there came the day when Angela gave me the most interesting news of all: "I'm pregnant". For Angela, being pregnant meant that she was to go back home, at least that is what her parents told her to do. She wasn't in school anymore, and given that the father of her child had run off, there was really no reason for her to stay in town, away from her parents. So, she left to go home, where she stayed until after the baby was born.

I saw Angela again about 5 years later, when I was in graduate school. The baby had been born, a cute little child with chubby cheeks and blonde hair like his mother. She was now a full-time mom, and her days as an aspiring doctor were far behind her. She worked in a local fast food restaurant, and even as a 25 year old, she still entertained dreams of becoming the doctor she once felt she was meant to be.

8

But life was different now. She was no longer a free-spirited 18-year old with her whole life in front of her. She was half way to 30, with a young child to provide for. Going to school was still possible, but it would be much more difficult than before, which is why she never took the steps to go back. Essentially, her ability to reach those dreams had slipped away, and she was stuck with a life that she had not envisioned.

# Lessons we can learn from this story

What can we learn form Angela's story? The lessons are very clear and pretty simple. This student started off as a brilliant young girl with a very bright future, and somehow transformed into something else over time. What you should have also noticed is that the transformation was not immediate or clearly visible. It was *gradual and took place slowly.* That is how life works. One day, go talk to an older person who has a job they hate. Ask them this question "When you were 18 years old, did you plan to be doing what you do right now?" 9 times out of 10, they will say that they planned to be doing something else.

You should also notice how as Angela experienced more disappointment, her expectations for herself changed. When she started to get disappointing grades on her report card, she eventually got used to them. The lesson is that you have to think hard about how you are going to deal with disappointment and failure. There are basically two kinds of people: those who use disappointments to inspire and motivate them, and those who use disappointments to discourage themselves and give up. Make sure you have the right response to the challenges in your life.

The final lesson to learn from Angela's experience is that mild and tiny distractions in college are the ones that can eventually bring you down. You don't notice it happening all at once, it just sort of happens very slowly. You are only young once, and those opportunities that you have as a young person are not going to last forever. With Angela, each passing year and every action led to her window of opportunity slowly closing. Before she knew what had happened, there was no opportunity left. The way life works is that the change you experience is gradual, hardly noticeable, like watching the clock move during History class. Do you ever notice how when you stare at a clock, it doesn't move? But if you do something else and look the other way, it has moved by the time you look up at it again? Well, that is how life works. Most of us just do what we do day by day, and things don't seem to change very much. But one day, we wake up and realize that we are no longer 18, but instead we are now 23. And a little while later, we are 30, etc. So, the only thing you can do is think about how your actions play into the life you want to have. You have to say "If I keep living like this every day for the next 5 years, where am I going to be?" If the answer is "in the gutter", then you might want to try something else!

# Random thoughts about life that you might want to remember

1) Time goes by a lot faster than you think. One minute you're 17, the next minute, your 35.
2) Working as hard as you can is always going to pay off, even if it just means that you are a tougher person.
3) Success in life is not always about how good you are, it's who knows you're good at it.
4) Potential means nothing if it is never realized.
5) Major changes in life don't happen all at once, they usually happen slowly.
6) Those who get ahead in this world tend to be those who know how to stick to one thing. Those who try to do everything at once usually get nothing done.
7) The VCR of life only has a "play" button. There is no rewind. Mistakes usually aren't easy to erase.
8) Those who are not afraid to fail are usually those who succeed the most.
9) Successful people spend much of their life as failures. It's their ability to keep getting up off the floor that makes all the difference.
10) A person that does not know how to set goals is usually going to live an unfocused life.

# What to do while you're still in high school

# Life goes on

Does she love me, or does she not?
It doesn't matter, cuz she's so hot.

I'm the man at my school, the king of the
court
I dominate every single sport

I walk down the hall, my friends just stare
Checking out my girl with her long pretty
hair

But after today, I'm no longer cool
Cause today is also the last day of school

My thoughts cut through my insides like a
knife
What am I going to do with my life?

I never had to think about that before
I used to only think about football scores

My counselor stares at me with a nasty glare
With his pop bottle glasses and balding hair

His eyes on my transcript are frozen and
stuck
He says to me "Son, your grades really
suck."

I remember hearing my father say
"Boy, you're going to get older one day"

I never ever listen to people that old
But now I can see that life's kinda cold

I can't live for free, now I'm paying rent
My pockets are empty, except for the lint

I don't drive to work, man I'm riding my bike
My fridge is so empty, my pet roach is on strike!

My high school days are now long gone
I realize it's true that life does go on

# As you finish high school

As you finish up your high school career, it's important that you start to ask yourself "What is going to happen next?" It can be tough to do that, since everything around you seems so important. But you have to take my word for it when I tell you that in about 5 years, that old stuff from high school is going to mean *absolutely nothing*. The prom queen is going to weigh 400 pounds and have greasy hair, the captain of the football team is now the local drug dealer. The school geek is now a multimillionaire with his choice of dates every Friday night. Life does go on, and even if you are not a winner in one part of the game, that doesn't mean that you can't win later. Also, just because you are on top now, that doesn't mean that you are always going to be there. Getting on top and staying there means that you have to have a plan. Education is the best thing to put into your plan, no matter what your grades are.

In this section, I am going to talk about myths of college, and also focus on things that a person can do to prepare for college. You have to get mentally ready and you also have to spend time learning the game so that you are successful later on.

# Funky college myths that you need to forget right now

### Myth #1: You can either have fun or make good grades, but it is impossible to do both

A person can make good grades AND have a great time in college, it's only a matter of proper time management. People get themselves into trouble when they don't understand <u>balance</u>. It's sort of like eating your vegetables before you eat dessert. As long as you do both, you are going to be all right.

### Myth #2: Everybody in college drinks

For some reason, many students are convinced that drinking is just a natural part of the college experience and that everybody does it. That is ABSOLUTELY FALSE. If you don't drink when you get to campus, then don't start unless you have a good reason. There are a lot of ways to have fun on campus that don't involve puking all over your best friends tennis shoes, getting killed by driving drunk or dying from alcohol poisoning. Also, most campus rapes have alcohol somewhere in the vicinity.

### Myth #3: It is <u>supposed</u> to take 5 or 6 years to graduate.

This rule tends to only apply to those who major in engineering, architecture or specialized programs. Even in those cases, 4 years is not out of the question. A student that knows their program is usually not going to have trouble getting out in 4 years, but those who do not are probably going to have trouble. If you were traveling across the country with no map, it would probably take you months to get there. The same is true with college. When you start college, learn the requirements of your academic program. You will then have a clearer path to the finish line, and be able to get there more efficiently.

**Myth #4: You have to be incredibly smart to make straight As**

Students who manage their time and work consistently tend to do very well in school, regardless of how smart they actually are. I have seen students with pretty low I.Q.s perform very well in my class mainly because they did what I told them to do. If you think that you are going to do well in college just because you are smart, you are in for a rude awakening. And if you are not the brightest student in the world, you can do as well as you want if you just put together a plan and stick with it.

**Myth #5: People in college are smarter and better than those who are not**

People who go to college are usually there because they are from a family that encourages its kids to go to college. The people in college are no smarter than the people who choose to deal drugs, live with their mother, or work in grocery stores. Where you go in life is about where you believe you are supposed to go. Remember: everybody has to work hard to get by. There are just some who are able to do work that pays a higher reward in the end. Education makes sure that you get more for each hour of work than you would if you had not made the same choice.

**Myth #6: Everyone who goes to college is going to make a lot of money when they graduate.**

How much money you make when you graduate from college depends on what major you choose and how much education you get in your field. Be sure to investigate all available options before you choose a major and decide on graduate school alternatives.

**Myth #7: A college degree is everything you need in the job market.**

The world is changing, and a college degree doesn't have nearly as much punch as it did back in the day. You should investigate to find out how much education you need to get the job that you want. You would be surprised at how easy graduate school can be compared to college. It only takes an extra year or two to get a masters degree, while college takes 4 years. Also, you get to focus on the things that you like instead of having to take the classes that they tell you to take. It's really not that bad.

**Myth #8:  You have to have a lot of money to go to college.**

Most students don't pay their own way through college.   Most of them use some kind of financial aid to get there.  Money should not be the barrier keeping you away from college, the money is out there if you take the time to look for it.  If you can't get scholarships, then at least make sure that you apply for grants and student loans.   Also, make sure that the school you choose is not very expensive.   It's how you perform that matters, not necessarily the school that you attend.

# The 10 biggest mistakes made by students who are preparing for college

### Mistake #1: Listening to someone who says you are not "college material"

The term "college material" was pretty much meant to keep the "haves" away from the "have nots". You are college material if you are willing to go to school and work hard when you get there. If you are not yet college material, you can be after you put in the time.

### Mistake #2: Waiting too long to take the ACT or SAT

You should get this over and done with early in your Junior year. Don't be afraid, just take the darn thing!

### Mistake #3: Not taking classes that will prepare them for college

You should make sure that whatever classes you take during high school are college prep classes that will meet the academic standards of college. If you are not taking these classes, then you might need to spend a year taking something else after high school to get up to speed. Don't be afraid, just make sure that you are willing to work hard every day to do well in your classes.

21

Even if you are behind, you are young, so you have the rest of your life to catch up!

## Mistake #4: Choosing a school that is too far away from home or too expensive

If you really want to go to a school that is out of state, make sure that you know WHY you want to go to this school. If you are comparing Harvard against some average state school, that is one thing, but if you are choosing some expensive school across the country just for the "hulluvit", then that is a problem.

## Mistake #5: Not applying to enough universities.

You should never put all your eggs into one basket. When you apply to college, you can't just send your app to one or two schools and hope for the best. You've got to spread yourself out there so that the world knows that you are going to college.

## Mistake #6: Not applying for every scholarship you can find

You should put your name on every dotted line that crosses your path. Serious scholarship searches can be very helpful in preparing financially for college. If you are not sure where to find scholarships, check the Internet. There are websites out there for foundations and other organizations that are anxious to give away scholarship money. You may also want to check my website www.boycewatkins.com, where there are references to available scholarships.

### Mistake #7: Choosing a school because your girlfriend or boyfriend is going to attend the same university

We all want to believe that love is eternal. Sometimes it is, but any divorce lawyer could tell you that it usually is not. This is especially true when you are young. But that doesn't mean that you should give up on your sweetie. It only means that you should be careful about how much you give up for this relationship. Choosing a college just because your boyfriend or girlfriend is there is one of those things that can make you feel really silly later on.

### Mistake #8: Not keeping their grades high enough in high school

When I was in high school, I didn't spend too much time worrying about college. I would either not go at all, or I figured that it would take care of itself. So, I didn't do what I needed to do to keep my grades up. That was a terrible decision that I eventually came to regret. If you are struggling academically, take the time to talk to your teachers about how you can improve your grade. Also, many cities have places you can go to get help with homework. You might also find that just deciding to put in a consistent amount of time toward school every day is going to yield good results. It's hard to do at first, but eventually you will get used to it.

## Mistake #9: Being afraid of the application process

The whole college application thing can be really scary. But it's not as scary as you might think. You would also be surprised at how easy it is if you simply go to the university or your high school and ask for help. You should be more afraid of what is going to happen to your life if you don't go to college.

## Mistake #10: Not studying for the ACT or SAT

Some people mistakenly believe that the ACT and SAT are measures of your intelligence. They are not. They are only measures of how well you do on a certain type of standardized test. You have to practice, and you have to study. At the very least, you should take 7 practice tests before taking the real one, so that you know what to expect.

# Secret Rules for students planning to go to college

### 1) Make sure that you visit the schools you are thinking about attending

You don't want to have to spend 4 years in a place that you hate. If a school is on your short list of possibilities, you should at least visit the location for yourself.

### 2) Try to live in the dorms, even if your parents are nearby.

Going to college is about a lot more than just getting a degree. It's about growing up and learning to be an independent adult. It's hard to do that if your parents are up your butt 24-7. Even if you attend school in the city in which you live, try to make sure you live on campus. It is not only more fun, but it will help you grow up.

### 3) If you move far away from home, make sure that you have money to come back and visit.

Going to college far away from home sounds really cool at first. But the thing is that if you are far away from home, coming back home is going to be very, very expensive. If you go far away to school, then you should either have some money available to travel home, have a plan to get some, or accept the fact that you are not going to be going home very much.

### 4) Don't choose a major because your parents want you to do it.

If you spend your life doing things because other people want them for you, you are opening a door to life-long unhappiness. Take the advice of loved ones, and listen to their wisdom, but always make sure that you are the one making the final decision. I can think of times when I let people run my life. I was never happy in the end. That was because their advice was not based on what was best for me, it was based on what *they* thought was best for me. Years later, when you've messed up your life because of what someone else told you to do, they are probably not even going to remember telling you to do that in the first place. People like to take credit for good things that happen, but not bad things, so make your own choices after listening to their advice.

### 5) DO NOT drop out of college for any period of time, no matter how small, for any reason.

Most people who have dropped out of school permanently did not plan to drop out for good. Most of them left school saying "I am going to come right back, after ……..(fill in the blank)". Before they knew it, a month turned into a semester, a semester turned into 5 years, 5 years turned into a lifetime. Do not put yourself at risk. Dropping out of school may solve a few short-term problems, but you could be creating a lifetime of regrets. For every million college graduates, there are several million "almost college graduates". You have to figure out how you are not going to end up in the group that never finished.

### 6) Apply to at least 15 different colleges, so that you can see what is out there.

Whether you think you are the hottest applicant in the world or the crappiest, you HAVE to apply to as many schools as you possibly can. You never know what opportunities are out there and what certain schools are looking for. You also have to make sure that you go to the highest bidder. The application process is not the same from one school to the next, so you never know who is going to see value in your application. Always create as many options for yourself as you can.

# Secret rules for community college and part-time students

### 1) Make sure that all your credits transfer BEFORE you take the class

Many students take classes at community colleges that don't transfer to the 4-year college that they decide to attend later. This leads to a lot of wasted time and frustration. Before you take anything, make sure that the class is going to transfer without a problem. You can find this information by talking to the counselors at the school that you are trying to get into later. Planning can help save a lot of time.

### 2) If you have a job while in school, be a **student who works**, not a worker who goes to school.

If you consider school to be a side activity, then you are not going to put it as your top priority. If something happens with the job, the kids or anything, school is going to be the first thing to go. Then, you will find yourself bouncing back and forth for years, spending 4 years to get through 1 year of college, until you eventually give up. You have to make sure that school is your top priority, since this is something that is going to build your educational, professional and financial future.

### 3) Draw a path for yourself on how you are going to get that college degree.

Remember the old saying: "We don't plan to fail, we fail to plan". When you go on a long trip, would you leave your house without looking at a map? How would you know which highways to get onto and not? The same concept applies when going to college. The students who are successful in college are the ones who have a plan and know what they have to do to get their degree. Don't rely on anyone else to draw the map for you, do it *yourself.*

### 4) Start your family AFTER college, not during or before.

Having a family is a wonderful thing. But having one too early can limit your long-run options in life. Family takes time, and the more time you have to commit to family, the less you can commit to yourself. In fact, some might consider it selfish to have a family and spend so much time doing things for your self, like going to school. So, if you want to create the best life you can for your family, you can do that by getting your personal stuff out of the way early. If you are done with your education and have created nice opportunities; your children will thank you later!

### 5) Don't settle for an Associates Degree, keep your eye on the prize!

Associate Degrees are cool, but if you can get more, then go for more. Once you have completed the 2-year degree, the four-year is not much further along. In most fields, the 4-year degree can lead to a much higher salary and many more job opportunities than the 2-year degree. If you decide you want a Masters Degree, you are in an even better position. When you set your educational goals, you should aim high. Anything can be accomplished if you put your mind to it.

# How to get ready for the ACT and SAT

### 1) Find a quiet, well-lit place to study.

When you are studying for any test, you should make sure that you are working in a place that is quiet and has lots of light. This usually means that studying at the kitchen table in your mother's house is not the best idea. You need to be in a place that allows your mind to really focus, like a library. If you can't study in the library, then go to a McDonald's or something, and take some earplugs so you can screen out the noise.

### 2) Try to simulate test conditions as much as possible.

Taking any test, especially the ACT and SAT is like getting ready for a football game. You have to practice in the same conditions that you are going to take the test. You should force yourself to sit through the entire exam in the amount of time that is going to be allotted on the actual test. Go through this process as many times as you can, so that when you take the real test, it is going to be just another practice for you.

31

**3) Make sure that you study a certain number of hours every day (with some days off every now and then).**

When you prepare for the SAT and ACT, you have to manage your time and make sure that you do something every day. Don't just buy the books and say that you are going to study whenever you have time. You should put yourself on a schedule where you put in 1 or 2 hours every day preparing for the exam. Treat it like a very important after school job that pays lots of money….you will get a very high paycheck from this labor in just a few years.

**4) Take as many practice tests as possible**

Don't just study the stuff that is in the review books, make sure that you take practice tests. There is a difference between the two. The review books might tell you what types of questions to look for, but taking the actual practice test puts you in a position to see how the questions are going to come at you during the exam. You should make sure that you do plenty of both.

**5) Try to take a Kaplan or Princeton Review course if you can afford one**

Kaplan and Princeton Review courses are designed to professionally prepare you for standardized tests that you are going to need to get into college and graduate school. They are expensive, but worth it. Do whatever you can to get a good score, since it pays off in the long run. But also remember that if you don't get a good score, it's not the end of the world.

### 6) Sign up for the tests early in your Junior year

Taking the ACT and SAT early is very important. You have to cover your butt in case you need to retake the exam. If you wait until your senior year to take the tests and something goes wrong, you are going to find yourself stuck with a bad score as you try to get into colleges. Take the test during the fall of your Junior year.

### 7) Retake the test if your score is not high enough, but don't retake the test unless you have reason to believe that you are going to do better

You may have good reason to repeat the ACT and SAT, but don't just take them over and over again to see if you can get a better score. Your score may actually decline the next time you take it. If you have no reason to believe that your score is going to improve the next time you take the test, then don't waste your time. Many universities check all your scores, not just the best ones. So, remember that ALL of your scores are usually going to be observed by admissions counselors.

33

### 8) Make sure you take both the ACT and SAT

Some students don't want to take both tests for one reason or another. But it is a good idea to have both of them on record just in case. What you don't need is to get into the last semester of your senior year and have them tell you that they need you to turn in an SAT score that you don't have. Having both tests under your belt can save you trouble later on.

### 9) Don't be afraid or let a bad score discourage you.

If you don't do well on the tests, consider trying again with a different study strategy. It is not the end of the world. A lot of universities look far beyond test scores to determine which students they are going to admit. You should not be intimidated by the tests, just determined to do your best.

### 10) Have the tests sent to as many schools as you possibly can

You should spread your wings as far as you can. By sending your test scores to a lot of different schools (they usually give you an option to have them automatically sent to the schools you choose), you are making sure that several universities know that you are going to be heading to college soon. This may lead the schools to send you information or waive your application fees.

# MONEY AND FINANCIAL AID

# The broken wallet

My friends laugh at me and say I'm a joke
Probably because I'm so dang broke

I'm broker than a window smashed with a ball
I'm broker than a tree with no leaves in the fall

My open wallet yells "Man, I need more!"
I'm broker than the glass I just dropped on
the floor

My money is cut like a lumber jack's log
I'm broker than the ten commandments
dawg!

I'm broke like a dude who can't pay his own
rent
Look Dr. Dre, I'm the REAL Fifty Cent!

Even when I was 12, I broke my own leg
It broke when I tried to kneel down to beg

My pockets are empty, so man can't you
see?
Going to college....it can't be for me!

The bill for tuition is 8 digits long
I can't make that much money without
wearing a thong

But people are talking bout financial aid

My cousin was broke, but now he's kinda
paid

He rolled up blingin, with 20-inch wheels
He was 5 foot 5 but looked like Shaquille

He told me that I can get money for sure
Without robbing and stealing or sweeping
the floor

But the important thing that I learned from
this guy
Is that NOTHING would happen if I never
try

Community college and state schools are cheap
There's no reason to slave and miss all your
sleep

So, keep this in mind if you want to achieve
There's ALWAYS a way if you truly
believe

# What you need to know about financial aid

As a Finance professor, you can guess that talking about money is one of my favorite things. Getting the money that you need for college is usually not very easy. However, you should NEVER let money be the reason that you don't go to college. There are many schools with very low and reasonable levels of tuition. Where you go to college is not nearly as important as how well you perform. So, a person that starts off at a community college and does extremely well can still eventually go to the Harvard Law School if their test scores are high enough after graduation. On top of that, there are many federal programs designed to help students find the money that they need for college. You should apply for financial aid and exhaust all these options. It is a very common myth that college is only for those with lots of money. Your future is at stake, so you have to make sure that you get your education *no matter what.*

# Where to get money for college

### 1) From yourself (savings)

Even if you are earning minimum wage, a healthy savings plan can put together enough money to pay your first semester of tuition at many colleges. Also remember that if you don't have a ton of money, you should probably not choose an expensive school! State sponsored schools where you live have lower tuition than private schools, so there is not usually a very good reason for a poor student to choose an expensive private school without a scholarship. I was poor, so I chose a state school.

### 2) From a part-time job or work study

Work-study and campus jobs are all over the place. Manage your time wisely, and try to find a position that will allow you to make money without having to give up your entire life. The best jobs are the ones that let you study while you work. You should ensure that your job has the flexibility to let you take time off to get ready for exams.

### 3) Getting a full-time job on campus with tuition breaks

On many campuses, full-time employees get substantial tuition discounts. I'm talking about people that work as janitors, secretaries, or other administrative positions. These tuition breaks might be your only means of survival in college, but these jobs can be time-consuming. You also don't want to be tempted to make this job into your career, since that is not why you are in college.

### 4)  From your parents or other relatives

If you've got parents or relatives with a little extra money, you may want to take up a collection for your college fund. You might be surprised by their willingness to help, or to at least buy you a little something here and there to help you out. You can also try going to them as an adult and asking if you can work out a loan agreement with them to cover your college expenses. They might be impressed by your maturity.

### 5)  Scholarships (athletic or academic)

There are scholarships for almost everyone. You just have to do your homework and look for them. If you happen to be good at a sport, stick with it and see if that sport can cover part of your costs. Signing your name to every application you get your hands on is also a very important part of obtaining a scholarship. If you are given the choice between an academic and an athletic scholarship that have the same value, I recommend the academic one, since you don't have to worry about being injured. Also, athletes have a lot of things to do outside of class. This can get in the way if you have a tough major.

### 6) Grants

Most states have grant programs for college students. Also, there are federal grants. If you choose a school with relatively low cost, you might find that the grants cover a big chunk of your total cost. Make sure you milk this cow to the fullest.

### 7) Student loans

Whatever grants don't cover, loans usually will. You should not be afraid to take out loans to go to school. Loans are a vehicle to get you to your goals, the same way a rental car can get you to work every day. If you don't rent the car, you can't get to work. So, taking out the loans is a good thing, as long as you only borrow what you need.

### 8) Your church

They're always passing the collection plate TO you, this would be a chance for them to pass it around FOR you. If you belong to a church, there is nothing wrong with talking to the leaders of the church about your financial needs for college. Part of doing God's work involves helping those who want to help themselves. You certainly are in that category by heading off to college.

## 9) The university that you are planning to attend

The school that you are applying to may have internal scholarships available that you can apply for. If you keep a good GPA while in college, you can usually find ways to get more scholarship money.

## 10) The military

I don't recommend this option if you are not interested in possibly going to war or dying to get your money. Most people kinda forget that joining the military means that you are giving someone else the right to use your life for means that might differ from what you've intended. But if this is fine with you, then you might want to consider the reserves, or even active duty. One of the ways they entice young people to join is by offering money for college. If this is for you, then you might want to consider this option.

## 11) Summer pre-college programs

Summer pre-college programs are sometimes available for students to help them get ready for the rigors of college life. These programs may also be helpful when it comes to finding money for college.

### 12) Jobs that have tuition-assistance programs

There are many jobs off-campus that have tuition assistance programs. You have to dig around a little bit, but a lot of companies are willing to pay money to help their employees gain additional skill. The kicker is that many of these programs usually require you to take classes that they approve. So, they may not be as interested in supporting a History or Education major as they are in supporting a Business or Computer Science major.

### 13) Internships and co-ops while you are in college.

Summer internships and co-ops are not only something that you should do to get the experience you need for the job market, they are also good ways to make money. The key is that you have to work hard to search for the jobs that might be available. Most schools have a career center that lists available internships, and you can also check the Internet.

# Financial guerilla war-fare (OK, we've covered the money part in general, but this is what you can do if you get REALLY desperate!)

### 1) Never give up

This process can be tough sometimes. So, you have to be tougher than the process. That means that you have to go into the situation ready to work as hard as you can to solve your problems and reach your goals. Never ever give up, because giving up is the only way to guarantee that you have NO CHANCE to be successful. You need your education, and you cannot let money get in the way of your chance to have a good economic future.

### 2) Tuition payment plans

A lot of schools understand that students don't always have the money right then to pay their way through school. Check to see if your school has a payment plan you can use to cover tuition.

### 3) Don't be afraid to borrow money

Loans are only bad if you are using the money for something silly. College is not silly. Don't be one of those people who never goes to school because they are afraid of having loans. That makes no sense.  You should be more afraid of not being able to get a good job or not having an education.  That is when you are truly poor.

### 4) Get your grades up as high as possible, as soon as possible

Good grades make it easier for you to get scholarships.  This goes for both high school and college.  Develop a consistent study plan so that some good university will find you appealing as a potential student.  I found that once I got into college and made good grades, I was able to get more scholarship money to supplement my income.  It may seem tough to make good grades, but if you put the same effort into it as you would a full-time job, you will be surprised at the outcome.

### 5) If you have to pay for yourself, find the cheapest school you can

Colleges come in all different sizes, with many different costs.  Don't choose a school that is going to break the bank.  If you are bright and can get rid of your money worries by going to a cheaper school, then go ahead and do it.  A great college GPA will open the door for you to attend one of those expensive universities when you go to graduate school (That is what I did!).

6) **Go to a community college if you have to, since they are cheaper.  Also, going to school part-time is better than not going at all**

If going to the least expensive school you can find is not the option for you, then consider going to a community college first, or going to school part-time.   The important thing is to always keep moving forward.

7) **Find a job that lets you study while you work**

Sometimes when you find yourself short on money, you may need to get a job, or even a second one. If that happens to you, your first pick should be a job that will allow you to study while you work.  Check for dorm monitor and security guard positions that might be available on campus.

8) **Consider moving to the state that you want to go to school in and working there for a while to establish residency.**

Most states have residency requirements, which allow you to pay in-state tuition (which is lower than out of state) after you've lived there for a while.  Some students move to the state the year before they start school just so they can live and work in that state and make themselves residents.  This can save a lot of money.  But you can probably do better by just attending one of the public universities in your home state.

# Your path to complete and total academic domination

## XBOX Blues

People wonder why I love my XBOX
Why I play it all night in my drawz and my
socks
All I can say is dang dude, it rocks
The game is my porage and I'm Goldie-locks

I play it all day, I mean games back to back
My friends say I look like a zombie on crack.
I'm hooked on this game like a big scoobie
snack.
GPA who?  Right now that means jack!

I'm bangin on Halo with nasty precision.
When I play SOCOM, we spank all the
missions.
I really don't mean to be rude with my rhymes
But I played with yo mama and killed her 3
times

As I shake that stick to make more blood spill
I notice sunlight creep through the window sill
That got my attention, I have to confess
Cause I hear my boy say "don't you have a
test?"

I look at my boy, then I moan and I gripe.
But he says "Hey, take another hit from the
Xbox pipe."
Then the pain of the test retreats from my heart
As I hear the jingle that plays when I push
"restart".

My conscience says I should put down the gun.

The test covers ten chapters, and I haven't read
one.
Normally, I would just let the test pass
But it's been like 6 weeks since I showed up in
class

Eighteen years later, I sell my old games for
cash.
It's hard to pay bills when you're picking up
trash.
My son is begging for XBOX 9 as we speak.
But I can't buy that stuff on 350 a week.

As I ride on the truck that stinks to high heaven
I reflect on my life as I turn 37
Where did it go, and what did I do wrong?
My mind weighs in heavy, like a pig or king
kong

College is not about being a whiz
It's only about handling biz.
The XBOX is no problem, though some think it
is.
Just save the game playing till AFTER the quiz.

If you jock the XBOX throw your hands in the
air
Or PlayStation 2, I really don't care.
I love my lil XBOX and I'll be gaming all night
But only AFTER I study, for I keep my game
tight!

## The secrets of academic domination

The secret to dominating in the classroom when you head to college is that *there is no secret*. The key is very simple: be consistent. That means study something every day, staying ahead of your class instead of falling behind. Students typically struggle in college because of a lack of discipline: Many of them have never had this kin of freedom before, so they let their work pile up. After a while, it's too late to have a chance at a good grade. The expectations of college are really not that great. Just do what the teacher tells you to do, and do it on a regular basis.

I am going to give you some tried and true secrets to doing well in a professor's class. As a professor myself, I have been surprised that there are so many students who do not know these simple rules. Doing well in my class, for example, is easy for those who know the rules, but very difficult for those who do not. The first set of rules are general, focused on how to get out of college quickly. Later, I talk specifically about how to do well in the classroom.

# Lessons for the "Get out quick" student (those who don't want to be in college with their grand kids)

### 1) Learn the path and put together a plan

Learn and study the program that you are entering and know exactly what you have to do to get out. Every university has a book you can ask for that describes your program in detail. You can also find this information on-line. Access this information and then learn your program *cold*.

### 2) Get those difficult classes out of the way and don't procrastinate

No class is going to go away just because you delay it. If there is a tough class out there that you need to take, go ahead and get through it. If you don't, it's going to only seem scarier for you later. Get a tutor if you have to, but get the class out of the way!

### 3) Don't spend an extra year in college getting another major or degree

Those extra degrees seem valuable and glamorous when you are earning them, but they don't mean much in the long run. Getting out of college and getting the first degree is what matters, not how many Bachelors degrees you have. If you have extra time, put that time toward a Masters degree, PhD, MD or JD. That is a much better investment.

### 4) Summer school is your friend.

Use your summer school opportunities to help yourself get out that much faster. You can kill an entire year of work and graduate in 3 years if you are diligent, or you can use the summers to make up for lost time. Try to get an internship if you can, and if you can't, summer school is your next best option.

### 5) Don't waste your time taking unnecessary classes: save that for the electives.

It might seem tempting to take this extra class or that one, but in the long run, you are hurting your chances of graduating. Focus on fulfilling the requirements of your program, which probably already gives you plenty of room in your schedule for electives. Taking a bunch of extra classes is especially bad if you are paying your own tuition.

# Top Ten Study mistakes made by college students

### Mistake #1: Thinking that you don't have to study just because you have no homework

Most of the work that you do in college is probably not going to be homework. Usually, the work is going to require you to study at home and get ready for some big exam or quiz that's coming up. There is ALWAYS something for you to read, study or go over, even when you have very little official homework.

### Mistake #2: Studying in the dorm room or with the TV on

You may not think that the TV is taking away from your ability to learn, but it is. Research shows that students who study with the TV on remember a lot less than those who do not. Don't catch yourself thinking that you are really working just because the book is open during the basketball game! You are probably not getting anything done.

### Mistake #3: Cramming

Cramming is one of the most addictive, but destructive habits of all college students. You should spread out your studying, not do it all right before the test. Cramming will only make your life stressful, miserable and risky. If something goes wrong and you don't have time to cram, you are going to fail the test. Also, cramming increases the chances that you are going to study as hard as you can, only to get a failing grade. You don't want to have that terrible feeling.

## Mistake #4: Not going to visit your professors

Going to see your professor should be a CRITICAL part of your academic plan. Staying away from them is stupid, because you are giving up the chance to get valuable help and information. Professors also tend to give higher scores to the students that they see and like. Go see your professors at least once a week, no exceptions. Also, try to visit them at least two weeks before the exam, since everybody and their mother is going to try to get into their office during the week of a test. During the week of exams, my office is so full, you would think I was giving a rock concert.

## Mistake #5: Not getting enough sleep before you study or before you take an exam

While you are studying, you should get plenty of rest. If you find yourself getting tired, you should take a nap. A fresh brain is the only kind of brain that can absorb, retain or recall information. A tired brain doesn't want to learn anything, and it is only going to make you dislike what you are studying. Push yourself hard, but be nice to yourself when you need to be. ALWAYS make sure that you get plenty of rest before you take an exam. Staying up all night before the test is just flat out stupid.

## Mistake #6: Only learning what the teacher gives you in class (not reading the book)

The teacher is going to go over a lot of things in class, but that isn't everything you need to know to do well on the exams. You have to find out your teacher's style for doing things, and then use that information to figure out what is going to be on the test. Usually, the teacher doesn't have time to go over every little thing in class. They are going to expect you to cover a lot of things on your own in the textbook. Keep a balanced approach to studying. The teacher is not going to spoon feed everything to you.

## Mistake #7: Not going to class on a regular basis.

You have to show up to class to get the information that the teacher is going to cover for the exams. Missing class is very tempting, but it is one of the dumbest things you can do. If you give in to the temptation to miss classes, you are going to find yourself falling further and further behind until you are unable to catch up with everyone else. At that point, not even Jesus can save you! Instead, he would probably let you

59

fail and then tell you that you should have studied.

## Mistake #8: Studying with a bad group

Studying with a pack of people all the time is the easiest way to get a bad grade. It can sometimes be good to work in groups, but most of the time, a group is the easiest way to get caught up in random conversations. All that has to happen is for one person to start talking, and pretty soon, everyone else is in the conversation too. Most of the time, you are best off when you study on your own. Groups only work if you are very disciplined. But being with your best friends at a table for 4 hours without talking is tough for anyone. A good group is one where everyone is disciplined and quiet. The only exceptions are when there are tough problems to solve or you have a group project. But even in those cases, you have to be the one to keep the group focused.

# CRAMMING

What does it mean to cram for a test?
Does it mean bustin your butt and doing your best?

It means risking it all, leaving so much to chance
Why don't you just go get your F in advance?

Does it mean aiming for glory to earn As and Bs?
Or does it mean caffeine injections through 14 I.V.s?

It means being all cranky and in a bad mood
And sleeping at breakfast with your face in your food

I WOULD say good luck or go break a leg.
But with 2 hours of sleep, your brain's a fried egg.

The doctor is in, and I'm not trying to front
But you ain't gonna pass if you ain't studied all month

You can't learn your math with MTV in your ears.
They'll say "what's the answer?", you'll say "Brittney Spears."

I've seen it happen time and again
They come to the door, and I invite them right in.

The weary-eyed student, with her hair in her cap
Her eyes red and puffy, with tears in her lap.

Her eyes aim to the floor and shift left and right.
Then she explains to me how she studied all
night.

I look in her eyes and then I just say
"Did you expect to learn all this hard stuff in one
day?"

I talk with the student, let's call her Beth
I explain that cramming's addictive, just like
chrystal meth.

"Your grade is roast beef, and you are the
butcher".
You just punk'd yoself, and I'm not Ashton
Kutcher.

I hear a knock a month later, for it's been a
while.
It's Beth once again, but she's wearing a smile.

The words seep out slowly, past the lips on her
smirk.
She got a perfect score, and it only took half the
work.

She's in a good mood, right after the test.
Cause even last night, she got plenty of rest.

She shows me her score, a 1 with two circles.
Her hair's fresh and bouncy, like a shampoo
commercial.

She's bright eyed and bushy with all of her wits.
Not like her cramming classmates, with stinky arm pits.

She got it together, and Beth is no myth.
Cause I don't call her Beth now, her name's Dr. Smith.

# How to take a test

## Rule #1: Jam, don't cram (yes, I am repeating this; it's that important)

Cramming is STOOPID. Yes, so dumb that I didn't even spell "stupid" the right way. You should spend your time studying hard early in the game so that you are not put in a position to have to cram later. If you don't think ahead, you are only going to set yourself up for serious disappointment. The students who wait till the last minute (to try to learn a month's worth of stuff in one night) are the ones who end up saying "I studied all night for the test, and I still failed it!" They are in that situation because they did not plan ahead. Instead of cramming, you should be "jamming". That is when you cram like crazy for the *next* test right after you finish the previous one. That way, you can get a heads up on the new material and impress your professors with the fact that you've gotten so far ahead of the rest of the class. Think of it like this: you are going to have to learn the stuff anyway, wouldn't you rather learn it early and get a good grade, instead of learning it later and getting something bad?

## Rule #2: Get plenty of sleep the night before the test (yes, I am repeating this too)

A lack of sleep only causes you to forget the stuff that you've already learned. Study hard the weeks before an exam, and then make sure that you get a good night's rest the night before the test. Not getting any sleep is like preparing for an Olympic marathon by trying to run a marathon a few hours earlier. That would be silly, because you would be too tired to run again. The time to prepare for the marathon would be the weeks before, and then you get plenty of sleep on the night before the big day. It is the same way when preparing for an exam, since you need a fresh brain for the performance.

**Rule #3: Don't miss any class the week before the exam, since important stuff is going to be covered.**

Missing class in general is a bad idea, but it's especially STOOPID to miss class the week of the exam. This is the time that the teacher is giving out all the inside information on the test you are about to take. Do not miss class for any reason.

**Rule #4: Go to every single exam review that is being offered, and go see your teacher at least 3 times during the week before the test**

If your teacher offers a review session, then make sure that you show up for it. Also, you should spend as much time as you can in your teacher and Teaching Assistant's office during the days before the test. That is what they are there for, to help you figure out difficult concepts. Also, they can see that you are working hard, and they will be that much more certain to remember your name and face.

**Rule #5:  Set two alarm clocks the morning of the exam.**

Relying on one alarm clock is just bad business in general.  Your ears may become immune to the clock (in other words, you could sleep right through it), you may set it wrong, or it may just not work for some reason.  If it plugs into the wall, that means that you are screwed if the electricity goes out.  The bottom line is that your teacher is not going to want to hear any of these excuses, no matter how hard you try to convince him/her.  Get at least two alarm clocks, both across the room from your bed, and make sure that at least one of them runs on batteries.

**Rule #6:  Don't eat too much, since that is going to make you sleepy**

Eating makes your brain tired.  You don't need a tired brain when you go to a test.  So, save the pancakes till after the exam.  Don't walk into a test on an empty stomach though, since it's hard to think about physics when your stomach is growling.

**Rule #7:  Make sure you know the location of the exam, what you need to bring, etc.**

The little details can trip you up and make the process that much more stressful.  Find out where the test is going to be held and when.  Don't assume that it's being held in class at the same time the regular class takes place, because the location can easily change. I often give exams in rooms other than my classroom in order to have more space.

## Rule #8: Try to find copies of the professor's old practice tests

A lot of frats and sororities keep test banks of old exams. This takes advantage of the fact that some professors give the same tests over and over again. At the very least, the old tests gives you an idea of what you can expect. As a professor myself, I don't agree with these test banks being in existence, but since they are……..

## Rule #9: NEVER leave the exam early…..go over your answers a million times if you have to

If you get two hours to take a test, use the whole two hours. The worst feeling in the world is to lose points over something STOOPID. You will want to smack yourself afterward. Go through your answers 2- 3 times to make sure that you did them correctly. If you go through for the third time and everything looks ok, then maybe it's all right to leave.

## Rule #10: Get to the exam at least 10 minutes early

Don't show up for a test at the same time the test is supposed to be given. Get there early so that you can find a seat and get comfortable. Remember: the exam day is the only time that *every single student* is going to be there at once. So, finding a seat is not going to be as easy as it might be during a regular class. Professors can sometimes start passing the exam out 5 minutes early so that students are ready to begin right on time. So, if you get there at the time the test starts, you will miss the boat. Also, don't sit next to people who cheat, it will only make you look bad in the end.

# General rules to help you conquer college

### 1) Choose a major by the end of your sophomore year

Don't rush yourself when choosing a major, but if you wait until your Junior year to choose one, you are going to cause yourself to be in college longer than you need to be. The Junior year is when students start taking specialized classes in their major, and you don't want to be caught without a major at that point.

### 2) Try to find a job that lets you study while you work. If not, then don't work more than 25 hours per week

Working while you're in school definitely builds character. But don't get crazy with it. Earn enough money to pay for the things you need, and then chill. Try to find a job on campus that lets you study while you're working, because then you can work 40 hours per week and it will also help your GPA.

### 3) If you have repeat options, use them all. Quality is more important than speed

Some schools let you retake courses that you've done poorly in and then take the bad course out of your GPA calculation. If your school allows

for this option, make sure you use it. Even if
your GPA is already pretty high, you can always
help yourself by getting rid of 1 or 2 courses that
are holding down your GPA.

**4) Make sure you know your academic
program and all it's nooks and
crannies.**

The first step to getting anywhere you want to
go is to know where in the heck you are going in
the first place. Figure out your path through
your academic program, and then set a plan to
make it happen. Don't blindly rely on hope or
the advice of your advisors, that is the quickest
way to get bamboozled. You must take
responsibility for your own success because this
is your life that you are dealing with, not anyone
else's.

**5) Try to get a good internship in your
field during the summer. If not, then
go to summer school. Make sure you
are doing SOMETHING productive**

Summers are not meant for slacking and
chilling. They are meant for doing something
productive toward your graduation. You can
still chill, but you have to be doing *something*
that is going to help you graduate from college.
25% of your life happens during the summers,
do you really want to waste 25% of your life
doing nothing?

## 6) Don't transfer to another school, unless you have a very good reason

Transferring schools is not for the faint of heart. It's something that you should only do if you absolutely have to do it. This means that switching schools because of a girlfriend, or just for the heck of it is not very cool at all. Once you've switched from school to school to school, you have to hunt all over the country to get your transcripts, you have to retake class after class, and maybe 7 years later, you've got a college degree! The quickest way to get through college is to find one school and stay there until they hand you your diploma. It's that simple.

## 7) Participate like crazy in class. Most students don't like to talk, so this is a great way to stand out in the crowd

Don't just go to class and sit there. If the teacher asks for participation, use this as an opportunity to distinguish yourself. Other students are quiet and afraid to talk, so this is an opportunity for you to show the teacher that you know your stuff. Also, it is a great chance to get used to speaking in front of groups. You are going to have to do this when you get a job, so you might as well learn how right now. Teachers are always impressed with students who participate.

# Secret Rules for Studying Success

### Study rule #1:  Keep track of the number of hours you are studying every day, and make sure you are honest

Keeping track of the amount of time you spend studying helps you to make sure that you are working as hard as you think you are.  There is no harsher truth than what we get from looking in the mirror.  If you keep track of your study hours, you will know if you need to work harder or not.  Also, make sure that you keep track of the number of hours you are <u>really</u> studying, not the number of hours you spend sitting at the table.  Keep the hours in a notebook log for the entire time you are in college.  Then, at the end of each week, analyze yourself and how hard you are actually working. I did this in college and I still do it to this day.

### Study rule #2:  Study in secluded, well-lit areas, not places that are loud or crowded

You need to be focused when you study.  That means that you want to find the most boring, quiet place possible so that you can concentrate.  Studying around a bunch of other people or in a place where there is noise is only going to force you to spend more time with your face in a book.  Be efficient with your studying and it will be over before you know it.   After you've worked hard for a few days, it will be a breeze to sit and read for 4 or 5 hours straight.

## Study rule #3: Begin your studying early in the day so that you can have it all done in time for the party

Get a jump on the gun and that will allow you to have all the free time to do whatever you want. *Going to parties* is not what lowers your GPA, it's the party that you go to *when you haven't done any studying all day.* If you start work at 8 am, you can have a ton of stuff done by 2 or 3 p.m., with the rest of the day and night free to shake your butt till it falls off the hinges.

## Study rule #4: Try to go over your notes right after the class in which you took them

The sooner you go over your notes, the more you are likely to remember them. Go through everything right after class, if you can, and that will make it easier for you when you have to go back through the stuff and prepare for your exam. You should also read the chapter for every class *before* it is covered in class. Think about it like this: you're going to have to read it eventually, but if you read it sooner rather than later, you are going to get twice the darn reward! Be smart!

## Study rule #5: Take a book with you wherever you go

You should always have a book with you, since you never know when you are going to have a bunch of free time on your hands. Why waste time standing in line at the grocery store or waiting on your friend to show up when you could be killing two birds with one stone? There is no worse feeling than wasting time that you could have used to get done with all the crap that is still waiting for you when you get home.

## Study rule #6:   Keep a lot of disposable earplugs in your book bag

It can be hard to study effectively with a lot of noise. You may think that it doesn't bother you, but your brain picks up every little sound and processes it. If your brain is processing outside noise, it has less energy to process what you are studying. Since you need to be focused, you should buy earplugs to help you study efficiently wherever you are.   Whether you are in McDonald's, in the mall, or on your break at work, there is always a way to study. The more studying you get done, the less you will have to do when you get back to the dorm.

## Study rule #7:  Jammin vs. Crammin

We talked about this earlier, so I am not going to go into it again. You know what to do!

## Study rule #8:  Never get lazy, never give up.

Laziness is the worst disease in the world. Don't ever give in to laziness, for a person who is a slave to laziness will never get to live out their dreams. It may seem tough to sit your butt down and do your work, but force yourself to sit there, and after a while, you will get into a groove, and your butt will become stapled to the seat. You have to work hard to get good study habits, and then it becomes easy to study. Self-doubt is a horrible enemy as well. This means that you have to find a way to confront your failures and not allow them to affect your self-confidence. Learn to dig and dig and dig until you get the outcomes you deserve. Nothing that is worth having is just going to fall into your lap. Great outcomes require hard work.

**Study rule #9: Always attend every class, get there 5 minutes early and make sure you sit in the front row as close to the center of the room as possible**

Never miss class. It can be tough to make sure you go to every single class, but missing classes is the quickest way to jack up your grade. You might miss a pop quiz, or some important information about the upcoming exam. Do not put yourself in that situation. Always plan to get to class 5 minutes early, that way, if something happens along the way, you are still going to be on time.

Sitting in the front row and center of the room is a good way to make sure that you pay attention, and that the teacher pays attention to you. Remember: you are going to be a good student, so you want the teacher to notice that you are a good student. The good student in the front of the room is the one that the teacher usually respects the most.

### Study rule #10: Make sure you visit every teacher at least once a week

Visiting your teacher is the easiest way to get free tutoring. Also, when someone knows your face, they are more sympathetic to you than if you are just a name on a piece of paper. Make sure that the teacher knows your face. As a teacher myself, I can tell you that the students who visit me the most usually get the most assistance with homework, quizzes, etc. Also, when you come around later for letters of recommendation, the professor is going to remember who in the heck you are!

### Study rule #11: Begin your day as early as possible

One of the best ways to study is to get it all done quick and early. If a person is disciplined enough to get up at, say, 8 am on a Saturday morning, they can have enough studying done by 3 or 4 to last for nearly the entire weekend. That leaves a lot of time for naps, parties and Play Station. Where people get into trouble is when it comes to wasting time sitting on the phone, watching TV, or just "chillin". If you are quick to take care of your business, you can have plenty of free time to enjoy yourself.

# Things that every college athlete needs to think about

# Strictly for the ballaz

The balla on campus has now just arrived.
I'll sign all your footballs for 9.95.

The cheerleaders and honeys all treat me real nice
My coach says I'm greater than Jesus H. Christ.

My head may be a bit swollen, like a big blimp.
But I deserve all these props cause I'm such a big pimp.

They even told me "don't worry bout class"
As they shake my hand softly and fill it with cash.

My hummer is blingin, with TVs in the back.
My 24s spinning, like my nickname was Shaq.

My diamonds are placed in my radio clock.
My system be boomin from way down the block.

The fellas get jealous as I roll through the spot.
Them fools always scheming to get what I got.

My girl is so tight, as she sits in my ride.
But she's not as tight as my girls on the side.

My bow for me like I'm an angel above
They treat me so special, this has got to be love!

About game number 5, I jump for the ball
And the defense hits hard, just like a brick wall

I leap from the tackle, "Man, you didn't hurt
me!"
But I fall back to the ground, with a crunch in
my knee.

I hear my doc whisper, as I swell up with tears
"This might be the end of your football career"

Now that I can no longer jump for the ball.
The coach that once loved me ain't returning my
calls.

I once got the line "Your tuition is paid"
I now get the phrase "Go try student aid."

All of my homies done got kind of rude.
They just look right past me, like yesterday's
news

As I watch my gold hummer get towed down the
street.
All I can do is stare down at my feet

I then see the joke, and I was the butt.
The coach didn't love me, man I was his slut!

While they lined my pocket with a few hundred
bucks.
Their dollars were delivered by flat bed trucks.

Did you ever take a second to think?
Why the coach's wife shows up to games
wearing mink?

While my mama is slaving as somebody's cook.

Thinking her baby's off hitting the books.

She goes Greyhound on game day, so her back
is in pain.
The coach and his wife came by private plane.

One hit, then pow! I'm in a chair with steel
wheels.
I bet the coach's son will never know how that
feels.

As the athletic department decides on my fate.
They then figure out I am only dead weight.

That is when I am shipped back to the hood
No diploma in hand, I'll be up to no good

I sit on the corner, as the summer heat steams.
I live in the bottle to wash away broken dreams.

Instead of the hype from scouts, fans and
coaches
I'm in my mama's crib, with mice, rats and
roaches

I once was defined by my strength and my
speed.
But I now realize that wasn't all that I need.

What would I change if I could press rewind?
I would work a lot harder to strengthen my
mind.

# The great opportunities of the American collegiate athlete

College sports provides a tremendous amount of opportunity to students across the country. If you have a talent in a sport, you should certainly consider using it to help you get an education. The important thing to remember, however, is that your athletic ability is a tool, not an end within itself. Like everything else in life, people treat you very special when you can do something for them. Great athletes get lots of preferential treatment early, and many make the mistake of thinking that they are invincible. I have taught at 4 major universities, and while I know a few guys who eventually played professional sports, I knew a lot more that never earned a college degree and have nothing to show for the years they spent in the lime light. You should use your athletic ability as the chance for you to get an education, and try your best to stay grounded as you go through the web of deceit that you are likely to confront. In the end, the only people that really care about you are yourself and your family. Never forget that.

# Rules for the aspiring college athlete

### 1) DO NOT let someone else choose your major

A lot of athletic departments attempt to choose the majors of their student-athletes. That's a problem, because they may likely pick the easiest major that doesn't get in the way of your sports schedule. You should have a problem with that because you are going to be the one stuck in a field that is not going to make you happy. The best thing to do is find out exactly how the program works before you sign with a school. That way, you don't have to suffer punishment for going against their team policy.

### 2) Find out if you are still going to be allowed to stay in school if you can't play sports anymore. Try to get it in writing

If you are an athlete, there is a good chance that the school only values you for what you can do on the field. That means that if you can't perform for some reason, or you decide to quit, you are of little, if any value to them. You must protect yourself in advance from this kind of thing. Make sure that whatever school you take an athletic scholarship from gives you the right to quit the team and still keep your scholarship. If you can't do that, then try to find a way to get your scholarship money from some other source (i.e. some kind of academic scholarship). You don't want your team to own you.

3) **If you have to miss classes, make sure that you call each teacher every time you have to leave**

If your sport puts you on the road a lot, you have to make arrangements with your teachers to deal with that. Some teachers can seriously have it out for you if you are never in class. Make sure that you talk to them personally every time you have to leave, to ensure that you are not missing anything important. If the professor is only getting emails from your coaches telling them what is going on, they may feel that do not respect their course. For example, I can think of a time when I had a football star in my class. Instead of telling me that he had to miss class, he would simply not show up. I would later get an email from one of the coaches telling me that he wasn't going to be there because he had to attend a "celebrity luncheon" or some other event. This did not constitute a valid excuse for missing class, and I did not take well to it. I was patient with the student because I could tell that it was not his fault, but as a result of missing so many classes for unnecessary reasons, he ended up not earning the kind of grade I think that he could have earned.

4) **Do not leave school for any period of time without a college degree or**

**guaranteed multi-million dollar contract in your hand**

College is something that you came to finish. No matter what happens on or off the field, DO NOT leave school for any reason or period of time without either a degree or an amount of money that is going to set you for life. Some people start to feel that they don't belong in college for one reason or another. Then they leave. Even if you don't feel that you belong there, make sure that you stay until you graduate. Then you can leave forever if you want.

**5) Don't choose a school just because they have a great athletic program. Don't transfer schools unless you absolutely have to do so**

There are other qualities to a school besides its sports programs. Make sure you look into the other things your school offers, like graduation rates or quality of academic training and job opportunities after graduation. Sports may be important to you, but you can't focus on sports at the expense of your future.

**6) Don't let your grades fall in the toilet, it will stay with you forever**

It's easy to get caught up in sports to the point that nothing else seems to matter. The TV cameras can make everything else become a distant memory. This mentality will haunt you for life, and you will be struggling long after the lights have dimmed and the crowds have gone home. I've seen students let their GPA fall as low as 0.0, and it always caught up with them. Make sure that you use the same work ethic that you have in sports to keep your grades up. It is very important.

7) **Learn your academic program well and do not rely on anyone else to tell you what you need to graduate.**

Don't let your academic counselors be the only ones who understand the academic program you are trying to get through. You need to find a way to learn your own program so that YOU know exactly what you need in order to find your way to graduation. Relying too much on other people is the quickest way to destroy your career, academic or otherwise.

8) **Watch out for creepy characters: gold-diggin women who might scream rape, friends who get a little too wild, or people who might be associated with gambling rings.**

If you are a big-time athlete, you're going to find yourself with a lot of new "friends" who seem to get a thrill from hanging with the athletes. This is fine and good, but you need to be careful around anyone and everyone you encounter. College life can get kind of wild, so you should watch who you trust and only trust who you watch. I've seen people get into a world of trouble for simply *being around* when someone else was doing something wrong. If something goes down, the police have a hard time knowing who actually did what. So, unless you have Johnnie Cochran as your lawyer, you may find yourself in as much trouble as the actual perpetrators of the crime.

9) **Talk to at least 4 other people over the age of 30 who have gone through the program and did not make it to "The League". They will be able to give you the inside scoop on how athletes are treated and what happens to you in the long run.**

The sad thing about the way the NCAA treats its athletes is that most of them don't know if they've been screwed until after they graduate. They get older and look back in time to find out that they were mistreated and exploited. You can learn a lot from talking to people who have gone through your program already. Don't just talk to the ones who had good things happen, talk to the ones who didn't make it to the pros. If you find that there are many former athletes bitter about their experience at your chosen university, that might be a sign of things to come.

10) **Use your position in the public eye for something positive. Conduct yourself**

**with class and remember that you are a leader.**

Don't be one of those athletes getting arrested every week for weed possession or drunk-driving. Be a leader, or at least a model citizen. The world is waiting for you to screw up, so don't let them get what they are looking for. We all make mistakes, but your position of power is also one that requires a great deal of maturity and responsibility.

# As the world turns and turns and turns and turns..........

# I Just got dumped

I'm moaning and crying like a chimp in the zoo.
My GPA is below negative two.

How could she do it?  I said in the end.
Why was she butt naked with my best friend?

The only question to ask is "Which one do I choke?"
Did she leave me for Stevie cuz I was so broke?

My lip puckered out in a tight little curl
Why am I tripping over this stupid girl?

How could this lady do me so wrong?
I yell and I whine like an R. Kelly song.

One thing you might notice if you take a close look
Is it's been like 6 weeks since I last cracked a book.

Why should that fact leave me so annoyed?
Cause she ain't worried about me, she's screwing my boy!

So, 10 years later when life has went on.
My GPA lingers, but the girl is long gone.

What would I have done if I had been smart?
I would not let my grades suffer because of my heart.

As soon as she did something so darn absurd

I would have straight kicked her stank butt to the curb.

The love stories of college are full of high
hopes.
But they are short and dramatic, just like the
soaps.

Have fun while you're seeking your husband or
wife.
But don't let that drama jack up your life.

# Rules for Life Success in college

## 1) Stay away from alchohol, drugs, promiscuity and gambling.

This issue depends on who you are. Some people think that a little drinking or sex in college is ok, some don't. The only thing that I DEFINITELY know is that too much of any of these things can be hazardous to your health or land you in jail. College is a breeding ground for all the little sins that tempt mankind. Enjoy yourself in college to the extent that you feel comfortable, but DO NOT get caught up in too much of anything. If your goal is to begin a lifelong career as an alcoholic, college is a great place to start. If you would like to catch some really nasty venereal disease, there are plenty to go around. If you would like to: get raped, go to jail, get addicted to drugs, or get really bad credit, then college is the place to be. I say all this not to scare you, but to let you know that freedom is always a double-edged sword: it is the chance for you to make your own bed, but in the end, you are going to have to lie in it. Be smart with your newfound power.

## 2) Watch out for the credit card sales people - only get one card at most, and try not to spend more than you can afford.

The credit card vultures wait every semester for those naïve, unsuspecting freshmen (with clean credit) to walk naively up to their booths. You have a clean credit history, and they want to offer you what looks like free money. If you get a credit card, be smart with it. You should only use it if you have to, and only spend what you can afford. Financial problems are a major reason for students dropping out of college.

### 3) Don't pledge until you are done with your freshman year.

Pledging for frats and sororities is fine, if that is what you want to do. But don't do it during your freshman year. Also, if you are having GPA problems, don't do it during your sophomore or junior year either. There is always the grad chapter! Frats and sororities are a lot of fun, but there is also the chance for you to get into trouble, or get hurt if you let the fun get out of control. Be smart with the choices you make.

### 4) Don't move off campus until your senior year.

Moving off campus creates a lot of new bills that will get in the way of your education. You have the rest of your life to live off campus. Stay on campus for now. It's not usually as cheap to live off campus as it might seem at first. Also, there is the added expense and struggle of trying to come back and forth to campus every day. Keep that in mind as you make your choice of where to live. You have the rest of your life to live off campus, spend the first few years living on it.

### 5) If you don't have a family yet, don't start one till you're both done with college.

Having kids is great, but not during college. Get your education first, so that you can use the benefits of that education to support a family. If you have kids and a spouse too early, you are going to be forced to either jeopardize your relationships with them in order to reach your goals, or you are going to have to give up your goals altogether. Raising kids is very very hard, and extremely expensive. It's tough to do all this when you don't have an education that helps you obtain a good job.

### 6) Leave your Play Station, Xbox or Gamecube at home. These are serious time-eaters.

According to the Journal of Personality and Social Psychology, students who spend a lot of time playing videogames have lower grades than those who do not. Getting good at video games takes a lot of time, time that you don't have when you are in college. Leave the system at your parent's house, or only allow yourself to play your games after you've done a certain amount of studying for the night. Having that thing in your room is only going to distract you.

## 7) <u>Never</u> drop out of school for any period of time for any reason.

There are a billion folks who have dropped out of school "for just a little while" only to find themselves never ever going back to college. Don't let yourself get caught in that category. Only drop out if there is no other option, and remember that even when you think that there are no options, that usually means that you just haven't thought about all the possible solutions.

## 8) Don't go home too much, you will never get used to your new environment.

It is always fun to go back home and kick it with the family. But the only way you are going to grow as a person is if you get out there, have new experiences and meet new people. I had a friend in college who felt the need to go home every single weekend. He seemed to never accept the fact that he was no longer in his parents' house, almost like college was just a place he went to work every day. You know what happened? He eventually flunked out because he could not handle the stress of being away from home. Now, about 14 years later, he has serious regrets about giving up on college. Get out there and live your life, don't spend all your time traveling back and forth to your parent's house.

# Secret Rules on Setting Goals and reaching them

### 1) Set long, medium and short-range goals

Goal setting requires that you focus on the long, medium and short-term horizons. Your medium and short-term goals should be pieces of the puzzle for you to fulfill your long-run objectives. Always make sure that you set goals. Your mind always needs to know where you are trying to go. A person without goals is like a sheep out in the pasture just living from day to day. You don't want to be a sheep. If you don't reach your goals, don't worry about it. Figure out what went wrong and try again. Try again and again until you start to get closer to the objective. If you are setting goals that are worthwhile, chances are that you may not meet them at first. But eventually, your mind will aim for the target better and you will find yourself improving before you know it.

### 2) Read your goals every morning before you begin your day, and then think about what you have to do ON THIS DAY to reach them.

You have to make sure that you keep your mental connection between the long run objectives that you are trying to accomplish, and the things that you want to do every day to make them happen. Years are nothing more than a series of days, so if you waste each day, you will end up wasting months and years. That means you would be wasting your life. You should read your goals every morning so that you know EXACTLY what it is that you are trying to do and how you are going to work toward that objective on the day that lies in front of you. Keep them written down and memorize them. Read them on your way to class, before you go to bed. Read them over and over until they are a part of who you are.

**3) Write down a careful long, medium and short-range execution strategy to meet those goals.**

Goals are only the first step toward making your dreams come true. You then have to devise a strategy to turn your dreams into reality. Without a plan, a goal is just a bunch of hot air. Put together your goals, come up with a strategy to make it all happen, and then execute your strategy day-to-day until you are ready to go. Setting the strategy is the second most difficult part of reaching a goal. The most difficult part is listed below: executing the strategy. I wish I had a nickel for every time someone set a goal and even put together a strategy to reach the goal, but did not follow through. The world is full of broken dreams and hopes. So you have to find out what you are going to do differently that is going to turn your dream into reality. It's like my saying "I am going to lose 40 pounds" (my goal). I then might say "I am going to lose this weight by jogging one mile every day and watching what I eat" (strategy). Those are words and I may have even written them down on paper. That might require some thought, but is not that difficult to do. The most important question to ask your self is, are the words going to become action? Think of setting the goal as having a dream for a new building. Think of the strategy as creating the paper blueprint for the building. Think of the execution as actually getting trucks out there on the construction site and following the blueprint to create the building. So, you have three things: the words, the paper and the building itself. All of these things are different.

4) **Don't be afraid to set high goals, just make sure you fully understand the price that is required to reach them.**

Everything can be attained by the person who is a) willing to pay the price to reach that goal, and b) aware of what the price happens to be. Many times, we lie to ourselves about how committed we are to accomplishing something. It is much easier for someone to claim to be the hardest working person on the planet than it is for them to actually follow through on their claim. Also, a lot of people get attached to the dream and don't recognize the level of hard work necessary to reach that dream. It is much more fun and glamorous to pretend to be Michael Jordan than it is to actually make the sacrifices necessary to become a Michael Jordan. Setting high goals is cool, but always be realistic when you think about what you have to do to reach them. If you honestly decide that you are willing to pay the price to reach that goal, then that is the goal for you.

### 5) Never be afraid to fail, for that is the only way that you will ever succeed.

The reason that great success is so rare in our society is because most people are afraid to fail. Failure takes away confidence, which makes you not want to try again. So, usually people try and then give up, or they never try at all. The path to greatness is usually paved with failure. You have to know this right off the bat. But the great thing is that if you can deal with the failures and keep pushing, eventually you will get that great success that makes all the failures go away. For example, let's say that a guy is trying to get a date for the prom. He may find himself rejected by 14 beautiful women. But if that 15th woman says "yes", then that makes all the failures go away. However, if he only asks out one girl and she says no, then he will give up and never experience the joy of success that makes all the failures worthwhile. When you start something, plan to pay a high price of disappointment along the way. Consider the price you pay to be the cost of the success that you will definitely get at the end if you never give up. The obstacles you face in your life will have a limit. If your determination has no limits, then you will always eventually win most battles.

### 6) Set goals for *every* part of your life, not just for school.

One important part of your development as a human being is that you remember to be well rounded. You can't just work like crazy on one thing and ignore everything else. If you do that, you end up being a geek who can't relate to people, or a person who ignores his/her family all for the sake of earning that extra dollar. The dollars are fine, but the fact is that you have to think about what is going to make you happy in the long run. One way to keep your balance is to incorporate your family and friends into your goals. You can have goals related to school, but you can also have a goal related to spending more time with your family, making new friends, or losing weight. If you have a relationship, you can set a goal related to making your relationship work or at least learning to be nicer to your boyfriend. Think about all the things that make you happy in your world, and work hard to get them all right. The actor Will Smith mentioned that not setting goals in every area of his life led him to have tremendous success on the big screen, but failures in his personal life. You don't want to have that same kind of pain.

### 7) Review your goals on a regular basis and think about whether you are doing what it takes to reach them (execution)

Earlier, I was saying that you must not only know where you want to go, but you must also have a map for getting there, and a vehicle that you are going to use. Keep checking the map every couple of days to make sure that you are headed in the right direction. You have to remind yourself of your goals every day, what the requirements are, and whether or not you are meeting those requirements. That is how you get to the finish line. This is a continuous process, full of trial and error. You are many times going to be down right angry at yourself for not doing what you needed to do that day. But at least you will have only wasted one day. You can then come back with a great performance the next day that makes you feel better. It should be a continuous feedback process, and you should be committed to it. Almost like kicking yourself in the butt and patting yourself on the back at the same time.

### 8) Never let failure get to you or take away your confidence

Many great people have strong confidence that carries them through the embarrassment of their failures. Remember that "being great" is not something that describes a person, it is a choice that a person makes. "Great" people are not usually born with greatness, they go out and get it. They make a day-to-day choice to go that extra mile, no matter what. They also understand that failure is just a bump in the road on their way to success. The more you can adopt that mentality, the more likely you are to succeed. It's like a gardening contest in a neighborhood. The person that wins the contest may be considered to be a great gardener. But it's not as if he is necessarily doing something that other people in the neighborhood can't do. He *chooses* to get up every morning at 6 am and water his plants. He *chooses* to read books on gardening so that he can keep up with the latest trends. He *chooses* to set goals every year to win the neighborhood gardening contest. He *chooses* to make gardening one of his great personal sacrifices. It is that series of choices that makes the difference for all of us. You should always remember that *greatness and weakness are typically a choice.*


### 9)  Be happy no matter what

It means nothing to reach your goals if you are not happy. No matter what happens, what you go through, or how things work out, you must ALWAYS find a reason to be happy and smile. We are all blessed with life and have many things that are very valuable to us: maybe it's our family, our health, the chance to go to school, or just having both legs! If you are ever having a hard time being happy one day, then imagine life with no legs or arms. That kind of image will probably make you feel better. The point is that no matter how bad things are, they can always be worse. Don't ever get so caught up in your desire to achieve that you forget to be happy. If you don't reach your goal, just try again, but remember that while you should take your goals very seriously, it is not the end of the world if you don't reach them.

# 10 things that college students do to ruin their lives

### 1) Sex, drugs, alcohol and gambling

College is a great place to pick up a lot of really bad habits. The worst thing is that people tell you that these things are ok. It's not that all of these are bad things to do, but at the very least, they should be done in moderation. It doesn't matter if you are in college: If you have sex with too many people, you are going to catch a disease or get pregnant. If you use drugs, you are going to become a drug addict. If you drink too much, you will become an alcoholic. Gambling can also ruin your life as much as drugs or alcohol. I have several dozen friends with really messed up lives to this day, all of whom started their downward spiral on a college campus. You should not think that because you are in college, you are immune to these problems. If something doesn't feel right, then you shouldn't do it. Be mature enough to make smart decisions.

### 2) Falling for the credit card scams and ruining your credit

There are no serious credit card scams in college, only the little people who stand out in front of the bookstore trying to get you to take their "free money". Credit cards are very tempting when you are in school, especially since you are broke. If you decide to take one, make sure that you are very careful with how much you buy with the card, and that you have a careful plan to pay it all back. Putting yourself in over your head can easily destroy your credit. That is not a good cycle to get into. Not taking care of your student loan obligations can ruin your credit as well. You should manage your debt as best you can, because if you don't, it can take decades to fix the problems that are created.

### 3) Working too much outside of school and forcing yourself to drop out

Getting a job in school is not a bad thing to do. In fact, it builds character. But you should work only to support your basic needs. If you find yourself working non-stop in order to pay for things that you shouldn't be buying in college, then that is when it is time for you to settle down and reconsider your priorities. Your professors are not going to care if your grades are in the toilet because you are engaged in too many outside activities. It is your responsibility to keep up in class. You will have the rest of your life to work, make money and buy all the things that you want. If you do it all too early, you are going to kill your chance to *ever* have the finer things in life. My mother used to say to me "People who work hard before they are 24 get to party hard when they are 30." I didn't understand that then, but when I was 31 years old bringing in the New Year on a cruise ship in the Bahamas, I understood what she meant.

### 4) Screwing up their freshman year

There are a ton of students out there who are spending every waking moment of their Sophomore, Junior and Senior years trying to compensate for the screwing up they did during their Freshman year. If you get off to a bad start, you're asking for serious trouble all through college. You will have to do 10 miles of work to get 5 miles of reward. Don't put yourself into that position if you can avoid it. The best way to avoid problems in the freshman year is to use a consistent study strategy. That means, you should set aside at least 5 hours per day in which you go to a secluded spot in the library and stay there. Make sure that no one else is around. You can do whatever you want for the rest of the day, but make sure that your studies get their proper attention. After you have done your class time and study time, you will have a good 5 or 6 hours a day to have all the fun you want, especially on the weekends (remember: there are 168 hours in a week. If you are in class for 15 hours, sleep for 56 and study for 42, you still have about 55 hours left for parties! That's a lot of party time!)

### 5) Pledging too early

The quickest way to ruin your GPA and put yourself on a downward spiral in college is to pledge a fraternity or sorority during your freshman year. Some frats and sororities are responsible enough to make sure that they don't allow freshmen to pledge. But even if they are not, you should not allow yourself to pledge until you've had a good freshman year. If you are still struggling academically after your freshman year, you should wait and pledge grad chapter. You will have the rest of your life to be part of the group, and you can still go to the parties and have lots of fun without being in the organization. I never pledged, but I had friends in every fraternity. The difference was that I didn't have an obligation to anyone, but I had respect for people in all the different greek organizations.

### 6) Choosing a major you hate or one that doesn't make as much money as you would like

You should not choose a major just because it makes money. You also should not necessarily choose a major just because it is exactly what you want to do. The best way to choose a major is to figure out what combination of things are going to make you happy in the long-run. I LOVE playing basketball, but I would not enjoy playing basketball for a living, since I am not good enough to make money at it. So, I play basketball in my spare time and I work as a finance professor, which I enjoy, but also pays the bills. You should choose a major based upon the ability of the major to take care of your long-term financial needs, as well as provide you with a job you can enjoy. So, don't pick something just because you love it, and don't pick it just because you have money or prestige. Find out what is going to be important to you in the long run and let that be the basis for your choice. You should also factor in what kind of life you want to have when you are older, say, 30, and how this job fits into that plan. Do you want to have a family? Well, they are going to need time and financial support. Does your future job give you that? Also, you should never let anyone choose a major for you. That is usually the world's quickest way to unhappiness. Instead, you should listen to the advice of others and then use that information to make a decision that works best for you. It is silly to not listen to your elders, but it is also silly to let them control your life.

### 7) Getting too caught up in things that don't have anything to do with academics

It's great to be involved with extracurricular activities, it is a very important part of the college experience. But one of the main reasons that students fail in college is because they get carried away with all the exciting things there are to do when you get there. The idea is BALANCE. If you find yourself doing too much of any one thing, then it's probably not good for you. Even studying is not good for you if you do it 24 hours a day. Your life is meant for you to enjoy, not for you to work yourself into a coma, drink yourself into oblivion, or play Xbox till your fingertips fall off. You are there for your education, and you don't want to ruin your GPA over something silly. Make sure that you manage your time properly and that you make others respect your time. If you are not taking care of things on the academic front, then everything is going to fall apart for you. The idea is very simple: just take care of your school work before you do anything else. After you've done that, you are free to do what you want. As a student, I had a nearly perfect GPA, and I had an *absolute blast*. I played videogames until the late hours of the night, I hung out with my friends, traveled with them all over the place, the list goes on and on. The key thing that I figured out early that led to my success was that I should put in my time with schoolwork early and then I would be free to do whatever I wanted. So, although I had a blast in college, the real fun started later, when I reaped the benefits of years of hard work. Partying is fun, but it's a lot more fun when you are a little older and have money in the bank (can I get an "Amen"?)

### 8)  Going home too much

College is a time for you to grow up and learn to be an adult. Don't catch yourself going home every single weekend. The umbilical cord that you shared with your mother at birth should be cut by the time you are 18. By going home too much, you are simply extending the cord down the highway. Visit your family, but don't spend too much time leaning on them. You will never learn to take care of yourself, and you will find yourself in your mid and late twenties asking your parents for money. While it's ok to get help every now and then, you are better off when you learn to be self-sufficient. Imagine if you had problems of your own and then had another adult asking you to take care of them? It would irritate you, wouldn't it? Well, that is how parents can feel sometimes.

### 9) Not thinking about going to graduate school

Any person with a Bachelors Degree who is in a field where graduate degrees have value should definitely go on to graduate school. The marketplace is changing, and the Bachelors Degree doesn't carry the same heat that it did in the past. You have to be able to compete with those out there with better credentials, and you are seriously hurting yourself if you do not go to graduate school. Your educational level can also have a big impact on your salary and job opportunities. Finally, the world economy is integrating, so you are going to have to compete with people all over the world, in addition to those in the U.S. You don't want to be left behind.

# All that other stuff that we haven't talked about already

# Extra stuff

What do I mean by "extra stuff"?
It's when you scream "I've had enough!"

Things that make you want to commit crime
Trying to pay rent when you don't have a dime

Trying to jog when you don't have your shoes
You wish you had green, but just got the blues

When all that you go for just falls apart
You think that you've finished, but you have to
restart

When you're making a sandwich, but ain't got
no bread
When the only way out is the hole in your head

When you're trying your best, but fall on your
face
When all that you do seems like a waste

That's life in your twenties, get used to it man
Cause the best things in life aren't put in your
hand

All that you get worth the grit and the grime
Will take lots of effort and getting covered with
slime

But after the slime is washed off in the shower
Is when you will see that struggles grant power

You're life is a journey, get your butt on the bus

And when things don't go right, there's no time
to fuss

Just get back up on it and try it again
For that is how a true champion wins

So, please let me leave you with this simple
phrase
Effort is torture, but hard work always pays

# Questions to ask your self when choosing a major

### 1) What do I like to do?

Never choose a job that you don't like. That is the quickest path to a lifetime of complete misery. My grandmother had a job for 30 years that she didn't like, and she regrets it to this day. She taught me that having a good education means that you give yourself the option to pick and choose what job you want, which increases your chances of finding your way to happiness. I agree with that advice 100%. There is also an old saying "Do what you love and the money will follow". While I don't agree with that statement completely, it does hold some truth. Basically, you are better at something if you enjoy it and are passionate about it. Think about things you've done extremely well. Think about a time when you did better than you thought you would, maybe because you tried extra hard, you didn't want to lose, or you were just getting into it so much. That great outcome is the result of having passion for what you are doing. A person that has passion for what they do is someone that is always going to go the extra mile. They are going to go above and beyond what is necessary in order to win the game, or accomplish the goal. They are going to be better than someone with the same skills, but less passion. Remember that as you choose your career.

**2) What are the factors that matter to me when I think about the kind of job that I want to have?**

Every one of us has our individual set of things that we know are going to make us happy. The key is to find out what is going to make YOU happy. This a tough job, since we usually confuse what makes us happy with what makes everyone else happy. We have friends and parents who are influencing us, and they are always promoting their own beliefs when they tell you what you should do with your life. Don't get caught in that position. Find out what makes you happy and find a career that matches that. But you have to make sure that you account for everything. How much does money matter? Does free time matter? Does prestige matter? This process requires a lot of soul-searching, and I encourage you to be honest with yourself, without worrying too much about what others are going to think (for example, if you really like money, then that is ok. Don't let anyone tell you that you are a bad person because of it, because your life belongs to no one else).

**3) How much time would I be able to spend with my family?**

Different careers require different amounts of time away from home. Some jobs, like Wall Street Investment Banking, could potentially make tons of money, but you may not see your family for long periods of time. This may not

116

matter when you are young, but it matters later when you decide to have kids. You may want to break your career into stages and figure out what you can do when you are young vs. what you plan to do when you are in your late 20s and 30s. As your life changes, your career should change also. If you were to, say, fall in love one day, your potential spouse may not be very patient with someone who has a job that keeps them out of the house for 15 hours a day. Being there for your family is a way to avoid many of the relationship problems that people run into when they are not available for those they love.

### 4) What is the demand in this field? Is it going to change?

If no one in the world wants to hire people in your field, then this may not be the way you want to make your living. The demand for people in your field means a lot more than how good you are when it comes to finding a job. So, you could be the best Dog psychologist in the world, but if no one sees value in your services, you are going to be essentially stuck. A good way to find out what is going to be in demand in the future is to go to your university library or the Internet. A simple search on www.google.com under keywords like "professions in demand" should give you plenty of good references. Do your homework when choosing a career, since this is what you may end up doing for the rest of your life!

### 5) What is the level of education expected in this field to be successful?

You have to know what level of education you should go to in your field in order to be competitive. For example, the Accounting and Engineering fields expect Masters Degrees. You can get along with a Bachelors Degree, but the money is not going to be quite as good, and you are going to miss out on a lot of jobs. The same is true for teaching. But some areas, like journalism, don't value Masters degrees as highly. Find out where you want to go, what kind of pull you would like to have, and what level of education you need in order to get into that position. If the field requires you to get a PhD before you can get a decent job, you may want to think about whether or not you want that much education. I got a PhD, and I am pretty darn glad I did it. However, I would be lying to you if I didn't tell you that it was a lot of work. But remember: anything worth having is going to be hard to get. Going through the struggle is what sets you apart from the pack.

### 6) What is my school good at producing?

Various schools have different things that they are exceptional at producing. Some schools produce great architects, and others might produce very good biologists. Find out what the strengths are for your school and if they lie in the areas you that interest you most. This may affect your choice of major. You can find out what your school is good at producing by talking to professors. You can also go on the Internet and find rankings of schools in different areas. If someone tells you that a program is really good in one area or another, ask for proof. See if they can lead you to some kind of ranking or tell you about students who've gotten great jobs in that field. Don't just take anyone's word for it. Also, if a lot of people tell you the same good things about a certain program, that probably means the program is pretty decent.

### 7) What can I do with this degree in case the field dries up?

The world is constantly changing. Sometimes the areas that are hot today are cold tomorrow. If the degree that you have has staying power, that means that even if the demand for a certain type of job goes away, you can use that degree to do something else. But you should always save your money and be ready to go back to school in the event that the opportunities dry up. When you choose a major, spend time making a list of all the different jobs that a person with your major could do. For example, a math major can be a math teacher, an actuary, a statistician, the list goes on and on. Remember that the major you choose may not be the first job you get out of college. You may have to find a "back door" route to break into your field. Another example might be Theatre. If your goal is to get a part in a Broadway play, you are going to meet a lot of competition. But someone who majors in theatre and also minors in business can not only sell themselves as an

119

actor, they can also sell themselves as someone who can help with the business side of theatre. Remember, anyone you work for is going to be thinking about the bottom line. Without money, they would go out of business.

# Top 10 tasks you should do in the summer (ranked in order of preference):

### 1) A paid internship to give you experience, preferably abroad.

Getting experience is critical, and it's always best to get paid for it. Having something international further adds to what you've accomplished. As one of my professor friends explained to me "People just don't look at you the same when you've gone overseas." Students with overseas experience are valued at a premium by potential employers. You can find these overseas summer positions and other internships by checking with the career placement office at your university. You can also look on the Internet. Doing a search on www.google.com under the word "internships" should do the trick. You can also ask your professors if they know of any internships in your field. They are hard to get, but you can get them if you look hard enough.

### 2) A paid internship in the U.S.

If you can't go overseas, there are a lot of good programs here in the U.S. Try to get with a reputable company so that it all looks good on your resume. The key to getting a good internship is to have good grades. So, this is another reason you should take your academics very seriously. The internship is the one time during college that you can get a job without having much experience, if any. You should also go to career fairs to network, this might be a way to land something.

### 3) Study abroad programs.

Study abroad programs are cases where you get to go to summer school overseas. If you can't find a good internship that pays, study abroad programs let you kill some college credits, have some fun, and also get a good international experience to put on your resume. They are also a great experience, since you get the chance to see other cultures up close. I highly recommend study abroad programs.

### 4) Unpaid internship in the U.S.

If you can't get paid to get experience, then get it for free. This isn't the best of the lot, but the bottom line is that having experience before graduation is very, very important. You can volunteer to work for a company, which would make the process much simpler than having to apply for a job and wait forever for them to get back to you. Also, since they are not paying you, that means that you can claim to work for this company for a while, but you don't have to put in mandatory hours. The best thing about no one paying you is that no one owns you. You should consider this option if you get desperate and can't find anything by other means. The goal is to get this experience on your resume no matter how you get it. Sometimes you can get experience with a much more reputable company by volunteering to work for free. You will get your money back in the long run, I assure you.

### 5) Academic summer programs that will help you get ready for your graduate program.

If you are going to graduate school, there are a lot of summer programs out there designed to help you get prepared for your field. Graduate school is a big step and a lot of things change, so it's best when you get the chance to see it up close before you step into the fire. Also, you can make contacts with other students and professors in your field. These programs usually run during the summer after your junior year, sometimes sooner. You have to ask professors and others to find out about the programs, since they don't usually advertise themselves very much.

### 6) Research position (paid or unpaid) with a professor.

If you are interested in research or the sciences, a research position with a professor is a productive way to spend your summer. Having a good professor back you is very helpful if you are trying to go to medical school or get a PhD. Also, working with a professor will be helpful when you are trying to get letters of recommendation. They know you personally, so they are likely to go out of their way to help you. Most professors do not think to ask an undergraduate to work with them for the summer, but if you are polite and creative, you can get them to consider this option. You may not get a lot of money going this route, but you should be thinking about the long-term effects on your resume rather than short-term payoffs.

### 7) Go to summer school on your current campus.

Summer school is a great way to propel you toward graduation. If the other options I've mentioned are not available, then summer school is a great alternative. Many classes are easier during the summer, so this is the chance to knock out a lot of tough courses. It's also a lot of fun, kind of a chill time where you can have the fun of summer and still stay in the groove of college. I had a great time in summer school every time I did it.

### 8) Go to summer school in your hometown while working at the same time.

If you can't go to school on your campus, then find a community college in your hometown that will let you take a few classes. They are usually cheap, and you should do whatever it takes to get closer to obtaining that degree. Check before hand to make sure that the credits are going to transfer, so that you don't waste your time. Also, if the job is not the kind that is going to help you get valuable experience, at

124

least make sure that they offer you a flexible schedule that is going to allow you to be free when you have a test or other important things to do.

## 9) Find a regular summer job at home.

This should be your last resort. A job should build toward something for the future, or you should at least try to do something else that is going to enhance your future. If you just take a dead end job that doesn't build toward anything, you are probably wasting your time. Only go this route if you absolutely have to. If you do this, at least be smart and save your money. You're going to need it when you get back to school. Under no circumstances should you sit around and do nothing. Taking a couple of weeks off is fine, but spending the entire summer doing nothing is a recipe for disaster. If you are smart, you will not let this valuable time go to waste. Remember: college is a time for growth, not a time for you to be stagnant. Enjoy!

# Things for minority students to remember

(please see *Everything you ever wanted to know about college – a guide for minority students* for a more detailed discussion)

1) **You are probably going to feel some isolation on predominantly white campuses.**

   Sorry to have to tell you this, but it happens. Many universities have not taken diversity seriously enough to make their campuses reflect society as a whole. This is especially true in California and Texas. Get used to the differences, but do not let them distract you. There are usually places that minority students gather, find them and find friends with a similar background. Also, seek friends of a variety of backgrounds so that you can learn something from them.

2) **If you are from a family without much education, you are going to need to have the courage to blaze your own trail.**

   Minorities have been excluded from the educational process for most of American history. Therefore, they are sometimes the first in their family to go to college. While there may be some who cannot appreciate or understand what you are trying to do, you should consider yourself a leader in that you are able to show others how education can enhance their lives. When I went to college

126

and did well, I saw that many members of my family followed my path. Being a leader means that you have the guts to do things that others cannot understand. They usually don't get it until after they've seen you go off and succeed, then they follow. That is what leadership is all about.

**3) Racism is everywhere, but most of the time, it has nothing to do with getting what you want.**

Racism is one of the strongest American traditions in existence. There may be people who don't want you to be on the campus, or those who might stereotype you in uncomfortable ways. You have to realize that none of this matters and it has nothing to do with your goals. Keep moving forward, and those who disagree with your presence will eventually learn that you mean business.

**4) Use your uniqueness to your advantage when it comes to getting scholarships**

Some colleges actually value diversity and have scholarships for minorities. Doing well academically can open a lot of financial doors for you. Also, if you are one of a small number of minorities in your class, your top notch performance is that much more likely to be noticed by the professor.

### 5) Remember that there are advantages and disadvantages to HBCUs.

If you are black, you should certainly consider attending an HBCU. Many of the institutions are very strong and offer a highly nurturing environment. However, you should also realize that this protective environment is not going to solve all your problems either. Doing your best wherever you go is the best solution.

### 6) Most campuses have an ethnic community, find out where it is.

Even a campus with a small percentage of minorities has a strong ethnic community (no matter what your ethnicity) if you pull everyone together. Find out where the other minorities are on campus, it might make you more comfortable. On my campus, the black students gathered at the culture center, and that is where I spent a great deal of time when I felt a little lonely.

### 7) Some minorities are stereotyped as great athletes, but you should define yourself as a great scholar as well.

Black people are the best singers, dancers, and athletes in the world. There is no shame in that. However, none of these tasks can be accomplished without the brain. So, to be great at one thing, you have to have strong intellectual capability. Show this capability in the classroom, for a strong mind is what is going to carry you in the long run.

## The grand finale

I think I've said all I can say
The next step belongs to you anyway

Life is weird and at times obscene
And you only get one chance to be 18

So while you're young please do your best
Your youth is the time for you to invest

Life will present you with twists and turns
The turns taste bad and the twists all burn

But in this life, which is a game
Most of the rules remain the same

Hard work, persistence, and courage ring true
No matter what in the heck you're trying to do

I can give you the nutshell as plain as it gets
You either grow old fulfilled or filled with
regrets

*PLEASE MAKE THE RIGHT DECISIONS!!!!!*

Printed in the United States
36397LVS00005B/415-552